percussion

essential Musicianship
for band

FUNDAMENTAL

ensemble concepts

Eddie Green

John Benzer

David Bertman

Percussion by
Evelio Villarreal

ISBN 978-0-634-09464-4

HAL•LEONARD®
CORPORATION

7777 W. BLUEMOUND RD. P.O. BOX 13819 MILWAUKEE, WI 53213

Welcome to . . .

Welcome to *Essential Musicianship for Band* and *Ensemble Concepts – Fundamental Level*.

Ensemble Concepts is designed to help you and your fellow band members learn more about playing in an ensemble. While learning the basics of playing your own instruments, these exercises will help your entire band or ensemble understand the important steps to making a rich, musical sound as a group.

As you play and learn from *Ensemble Concepts*, it's important to:

 LISTEN carefully to your own
sounds and to those around you.

 FOLLOW your director's suggestions as you
work on the goals listed with each exercise.

 STRIVE to do your part to improve the
sound of the entire band or ensemble.

 REMEMBER that a good musical group is the result
of all its players working together like a team.

 ENJOY the great sounds that come from a music
group that likes to learn and perform together.

The skills learned in *Ensemble Concepts* will prepare you and your ensemble for all the great music that awaits you. As you progress, you'll be amazed how enjoyable and rewarding playing an instrument in a group can be, whether it's band, orchestra, or just a small group with friends.

Good luck and have fun with all your music experiences!

HAL•LEONARD®

1. Ensemble Sound

1-1 Full Band – Concert F

Counting Review
1. Counting, foot-tapping and using a metronome helps maintain a steady beat.
2. Tap your foot down on each number and up on each "&".

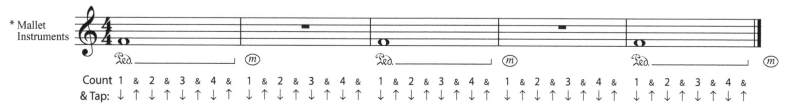

Count 1 & 2 & 3 & 4 & 1 & 2 & 3 & 4 & 1 & 2 & 3 & 4 & 1 & 2 & 3 & 4 & 1 & 2 & 3 & 4 &
& Tap: ↓ ↑

*Xylophone, Bells, Marimba, Vibes
Ped. (Vibes only)

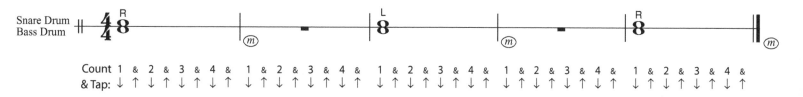

Count 1 & 2 & 3 & 4 & 1 & 2 & 3 & 4 & 1 & 2 & 3 & 4 & 1 & 2 & 3 & 4 & 1 & 2 & 3 & 4 &
& Tap: ↓ ↑

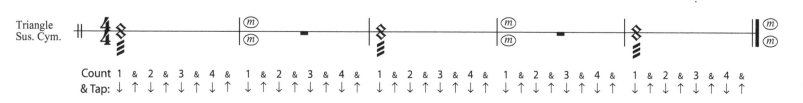

Count 1 & 2 & 3 & 4 & 1 & 2 & 3 & 4 & 1 & 2 & 3 & 4 & 1 & 2 & 3 & 4 & 1 & 2 & 3 & 4 &
& Tap: ↓ ↑

ⓜ = Muffle (dampen)

 Percussion Goals
1. Breathe together.
2. Start together.
3. Strike the instrument in the same place with the same energy every time.

1-2 Matching Sections – Concert F

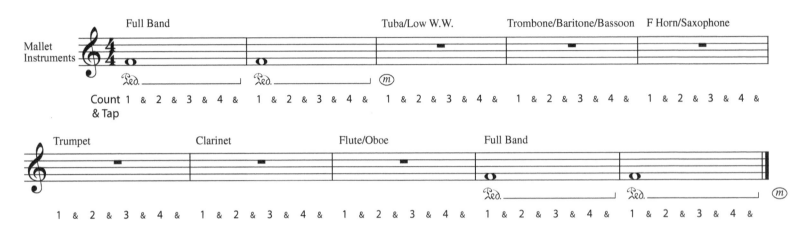

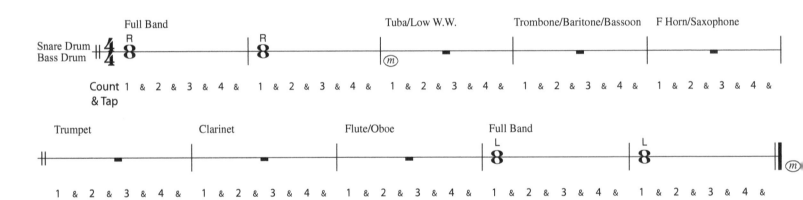

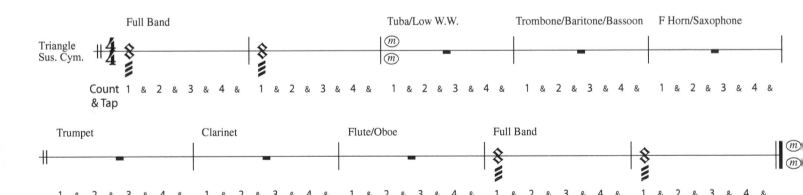

 Percussion Goals

1. Breathe together.
2. Start together.
3. Strike the instrument in the same place
   with the same energy every time.

2. Rhythm and Tonguing Exercises

2-1 Long to Short Notes

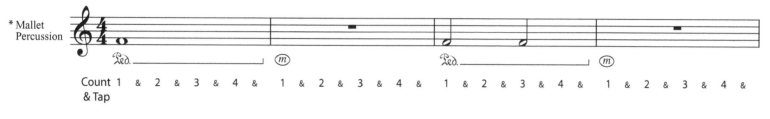

* Mallet
Percussion

Count 1 & 2 & 3 & 4 & 1 & 2 & 3 & 4 & 1 & 2 & 3 & 4 & 1 & 2 & 3 & 4 &
& Tap

1 & 2 & 3 & 4 & 1 & 2 & 3 & 4 & 1 & 2 & 3 & 4 & 1 & 2 & 3 & 4 &

* Xylophone, Bells, Marimba, Vibes
Ped. (Vibes only)

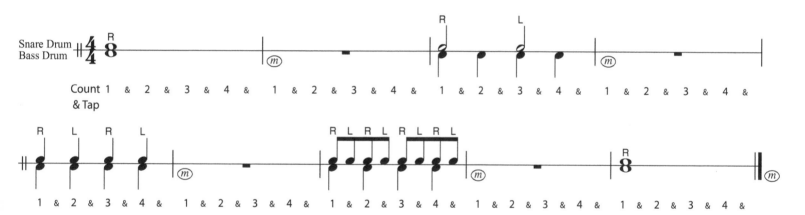

Snare Drum
Bass Drum

Count 1 & 2 & 3 & 4 & 1 & 2 & 3 & 4 & 1 & 2 & 3 & 4 & 1 & 2 & 3 & 4 &
& Tap

1 & 2 & 3 & 4 & 1 & 2 & 3 & 4 & 1 & 2 & 3 & 4 & 1 & 2 & 3 & 4 & 1 & 2 & 3 & 4 &

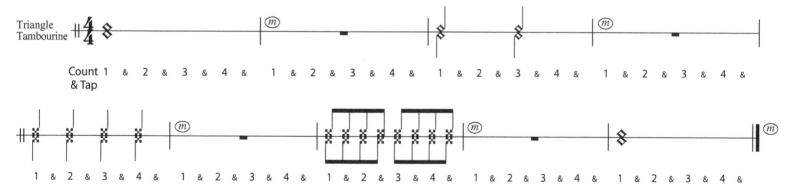

Triangle
Tambourine

Count 1 & 2 & 3 & 4 & 1 & 2 & 3 & 4 & 1 & 2 & 3 & 4 & 1 & 2 & 3 & 4 &
& Tap

1 & 2 & 3 & 4 & 1 & 2 & 3 & 4 & 1 & 2 & 3 & 4 & 1 & 2 & 3 & 4 & 1 & 2 & 3 & 4 &

ⓜ = Muffle (dampen)

Percussion Goals
1. Start together.
2. Strike the instrument in the same place
   with the same energy every time.
3. The quicker the notes, the smoother
   the mallet/stick motion should look.

2-2 Short to Long Notes

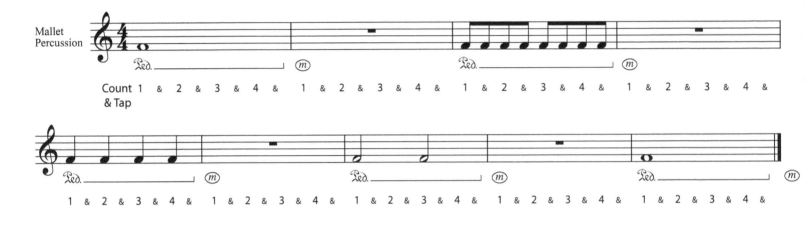

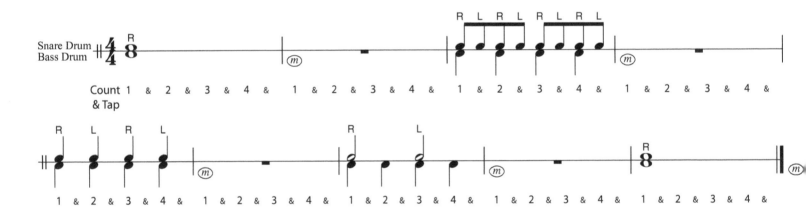

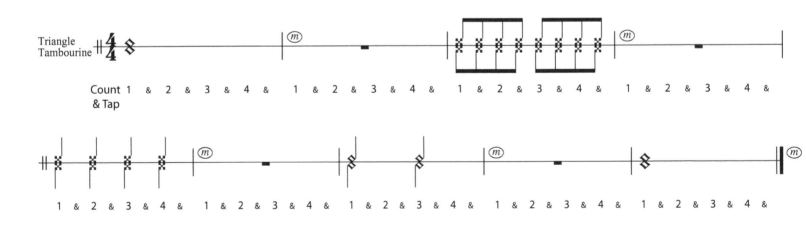

Percussion Goals
1. Start together.
2. Strike the instrument in the same place with the same energy every time.
3. The quicker the notes, the smoother the mallet/stick motion should look.

2-3 Long to Short Notes

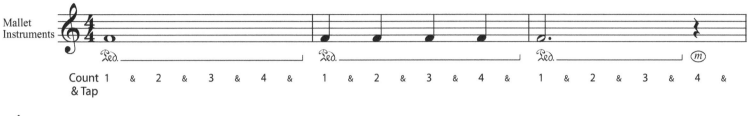

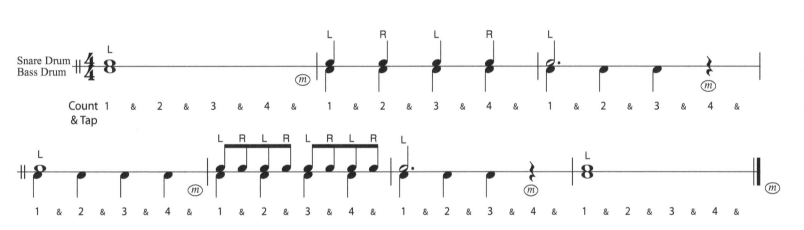

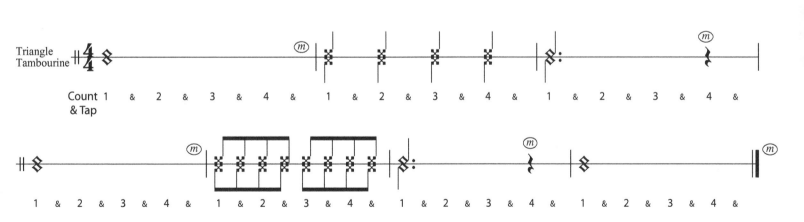

Percussion Goals

1. Start together.
2. Strike the instrument in the same place with the same energy every time.
3. The quicker the notes, the smoother the mallet/stick motion should look.

2-4 Short to Long Notes

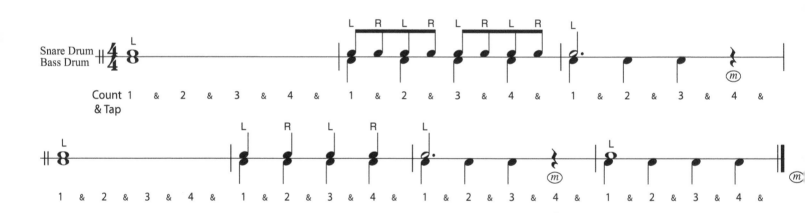

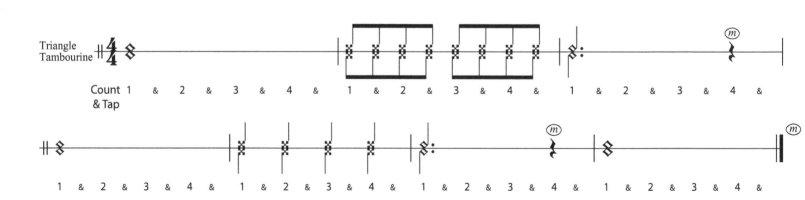

 Percussion Goals
1. Start together.
2. Strike the instrument in the same place with the same energy every time.
3. The quicker the notes, the smoother the mallet/stick motion should look.

3. Moving Steps (Intervals)

3-1 Moving Steps Down

* Mallet Instruments

* Xylophone, Bells, Marimba, Vibes
𝄢 (Vibes only)

Snare Drum
Bass Drum

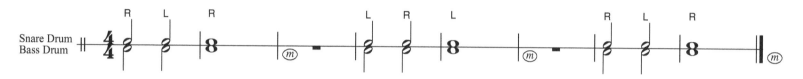

Triangle
Sus. Cym.

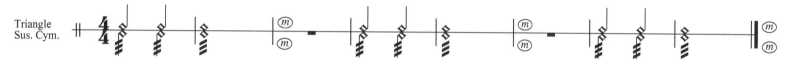

 = Muffle (dampen)

Percussion Goals
1. Breathe together and start together.
2. Strike the instrument in the same place with the same energy every time.
3. Dampen to match the ends of the wind players' notes.

3-2 Moving Steps Up

Mallet Instruments

Snare Drum
Bass Drum

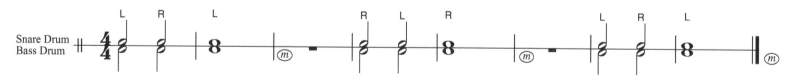

Triangle
Sus. Cym.

Percussion Goals
1. Breathe together and start together.
2. Strike the instrument in the same place with the same energy every time.
3. Dampen to match the ends of the wind players' notes.

3-3 Moving Steps Up and Down

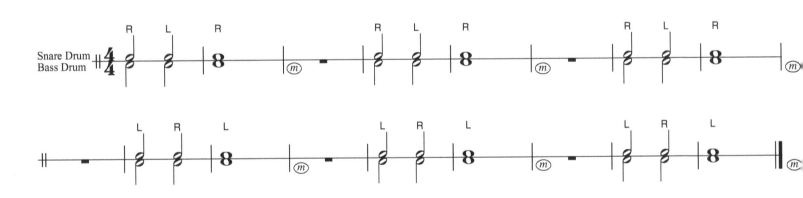

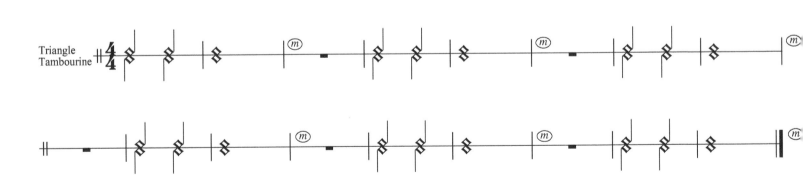

Percussion Goals
1. Breathe together and start together.
2. Strike the instrument in the same place
   with the same energy every time.
3. Dampen to match the ends of the wind players' notes.

4. Tonguing and Slurring

4-1 Half Steps Moving Down

* Xylophone, Bells, Marimba, Vibes
🎵 (Vibes only)

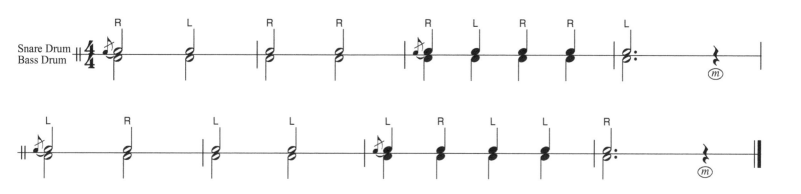

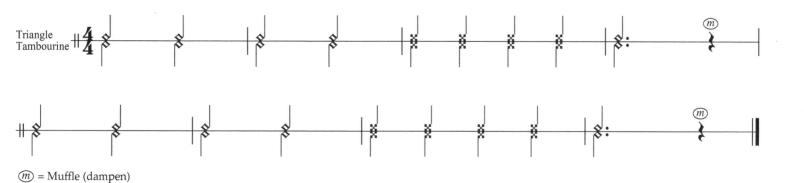

ⓜ = Muffle (dampen)

 Percussion Goals
1. Breathe together and start together.
2. Strike the instrument in the same place with the same energy every time.
3. Dampen to match the ends of the wind players' notes.

4-2 Whole Steps Moving Down

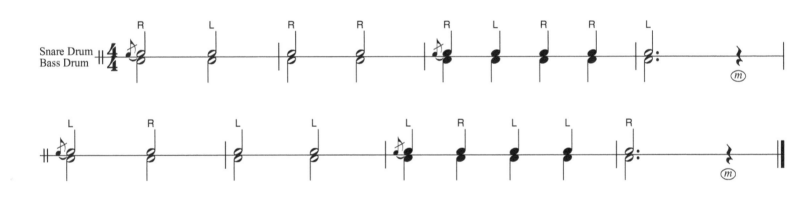

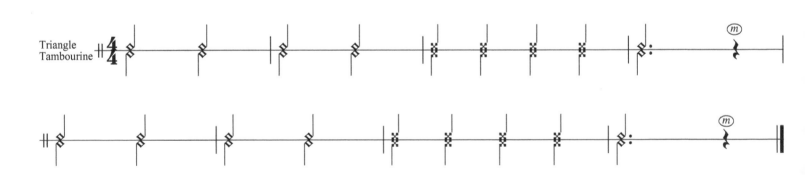

Percussion Goals

1. Breathe together and start together.
2. Strike the instrument in the same place
   with the same energy every time.
3. Dampen to match the ends of the wind players' notes.

4-3 Thirds Moving Down

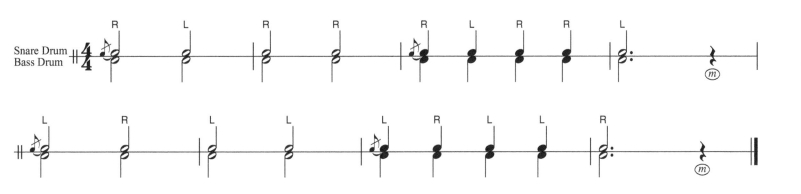

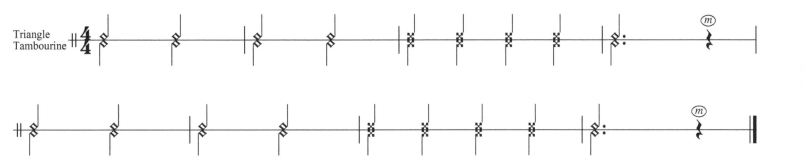

Percussion Goals
1. Breathe together and start together.
2. Strike the instrument in the same place
   with the same energy every time.
3. Dampen to match the ends of the wind players' notes.

4-4 Half Steps Moving Up

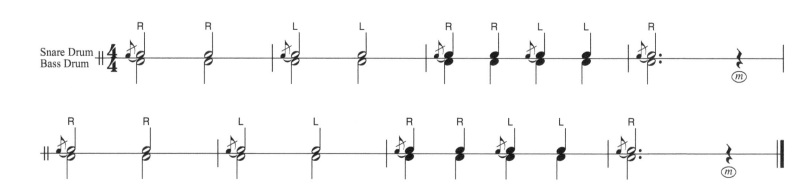

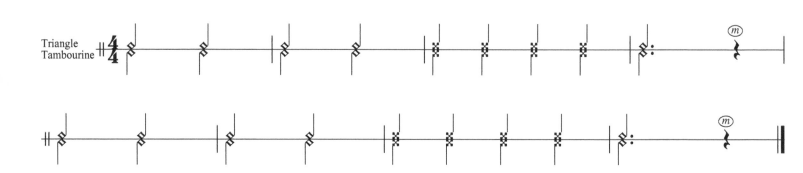

 Percussion Goals

1. Breathe together and start together.
2. Strike the instrument in the same place
   with the same energy every time.
3. Dampen to match the ends of the wind players' notes.

4-5 Whole Steps Moving Up

Mallet Instruments

Rolls for Xylo./Mar. only

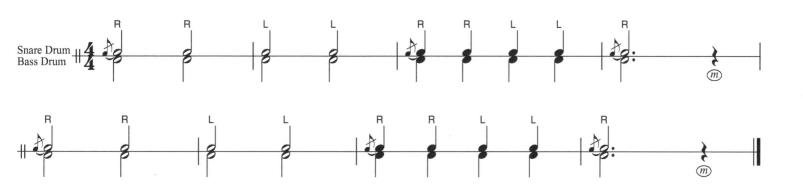

Snare Drum
Bass Drum

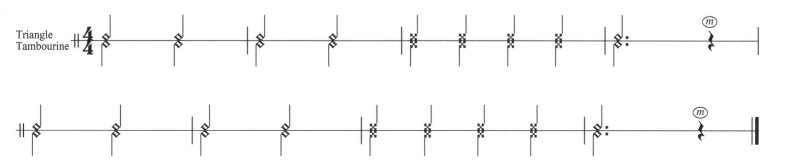

Triangle
Tambourine

Percussion Goals

1. Breathe together and start together.
2. Strike the instrument in the same place with the same energy every time.
3. Dampen to match the ends of the wind players' notes.

4-6 Thirds Moving Up

Mallet Instruments

Rolls for Xylo./Mar. only

Snare Drum
Bass Drum

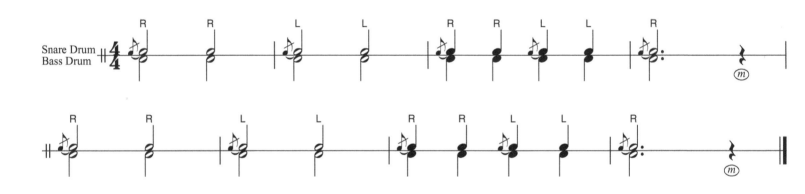

Triangle
Tambourine

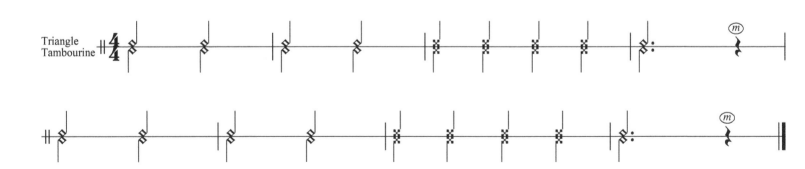

Percussion Goals
1. Breathe together and start together.
2. Strike the instrument in the same place
   with the same energy every time.
3. Dampen to match the ends of the wind players' notes.

4-7 Fifths Moving Down (Whole Notes)

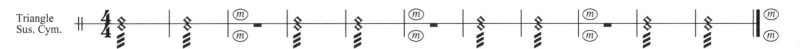

 Percussion Goals
1. Breathe together and start together.
2. Dampen to match the ends of the wind players' notes.
3. Match the volume of the winds.

4-8 Fifths Moving Down (Half Notes)

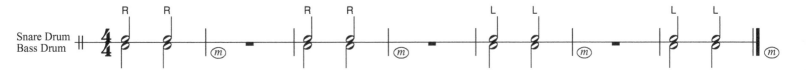

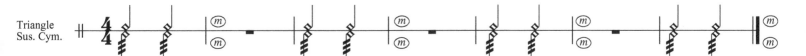

 Percussion Goals
1. Breathe together and start together.
2. Dampen to match the ends of the wind players' notes.
3. Match the volume of the winds.

4-9 Fifths Moving Up (Whole Notes)

Percussion Goals

1. Breathe together and start together.
2. Dampen to match the ends of the wind players' notes.
3. Match the volume of the winds.

4-10 Fifths Moving Up (Half Notes)

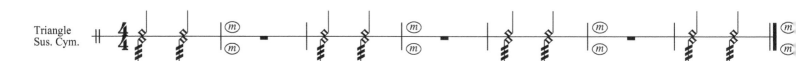

Percussion Goals

1. Breathe together and start together.
2. Dampen to match the ends of the wind players' notes.
3. Match the volume of the winds.

4-11 Fifths Moving Down and Up

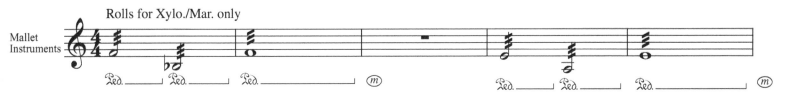

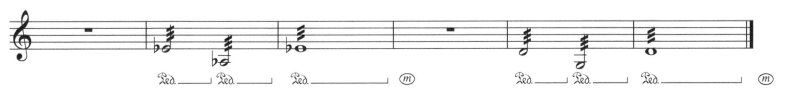

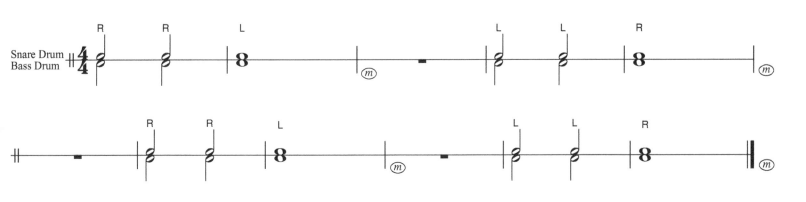

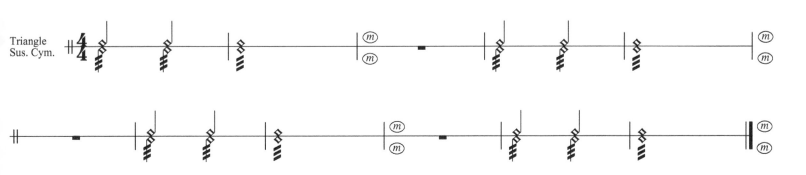

 ## Percussion Goals

1. Breathe together and start together.
2. Dampen to match the ends of the wind players' notes.
3. Match the volume of the winds.

5. Scale Steps

5-1 Moving Down (Tonguing and Slurring)

* Xylophone, Bells, Marimba, Vibes

🎹. (Vibes only)

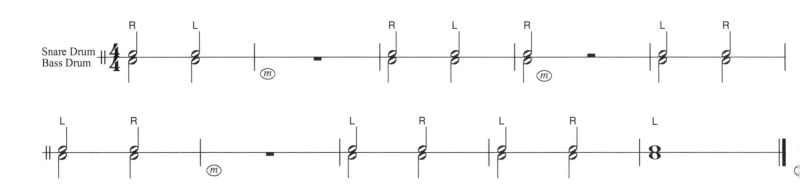

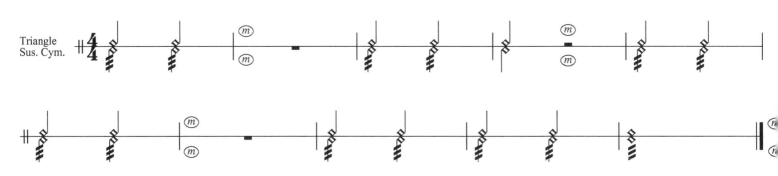

 = Muffle (dampen)

✔ Percussion Goals
1. Breathe together and start together.
2. Match the volume of the winds.
3. Posture should be natural with the body position balanced.

5-2 Moving Up (Tonguing and Slurring)

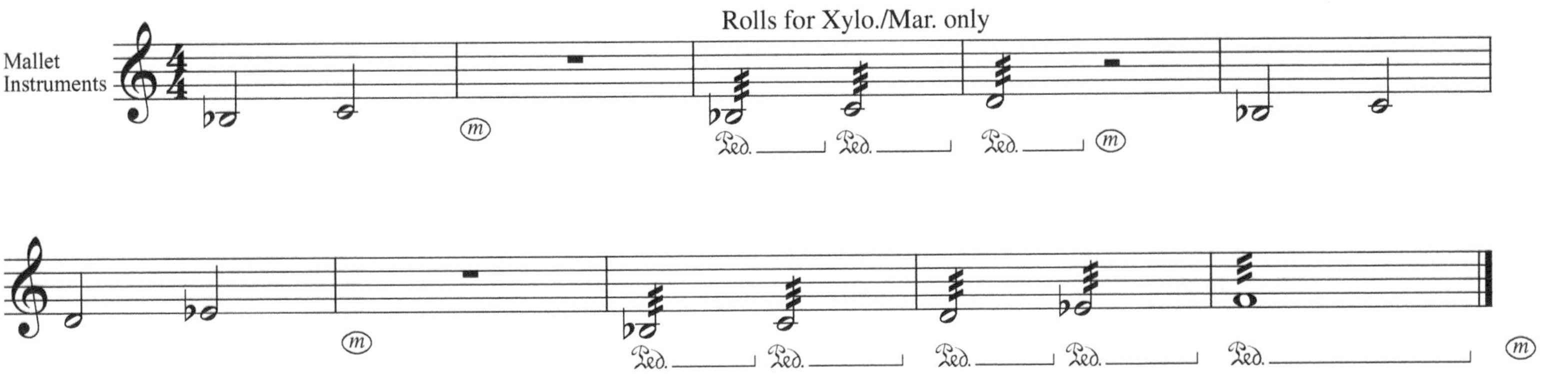

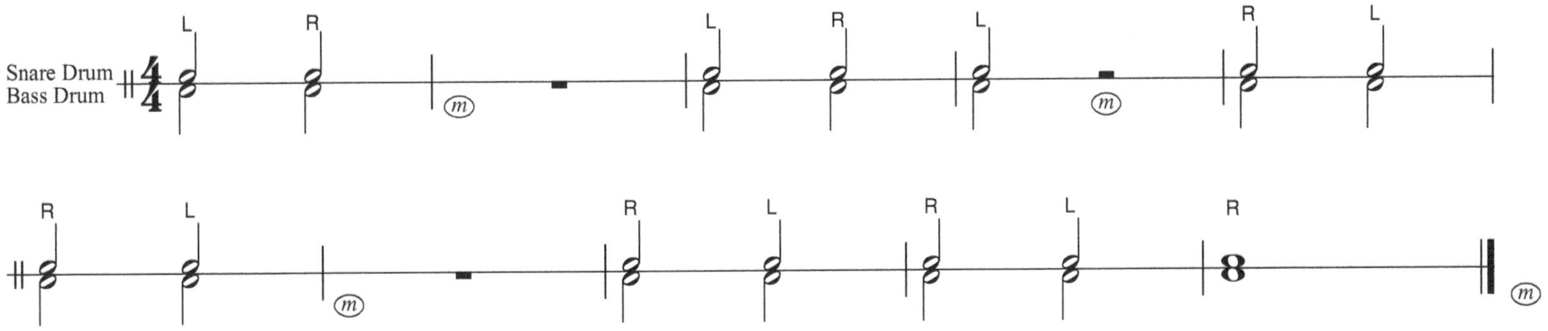

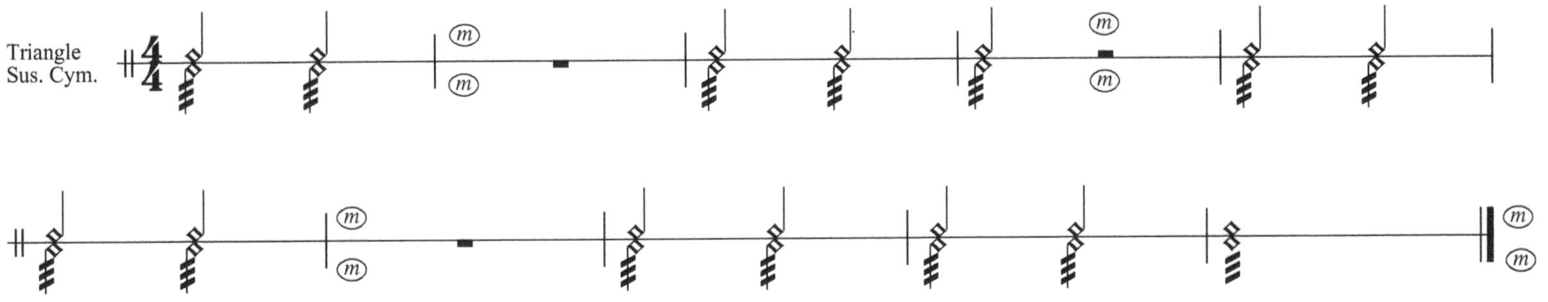

Percussion Goals

1. Breathe together and start together.
2. Match the volume of the winds.
3. Posture should be natural with the body position balanced.

5-3 Moving Down (Slurring and Tonguing)

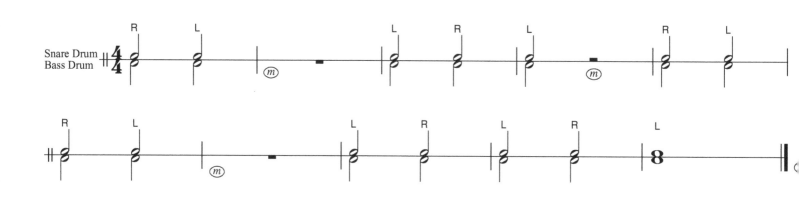

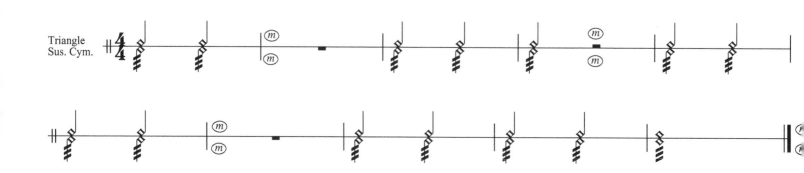

Percussion Goals
1. Breathe together and start together.
2. Match the volume of the winds.
3. Posture should be natural with the body position balanced.

5-4 Moving Up (Slurring and Tonguing)

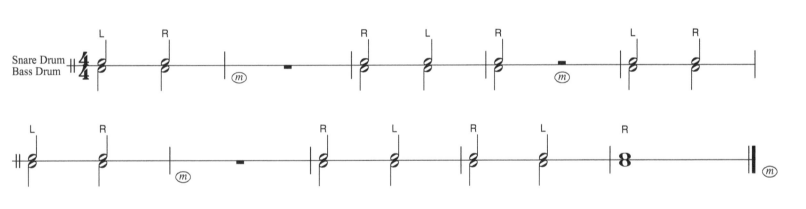

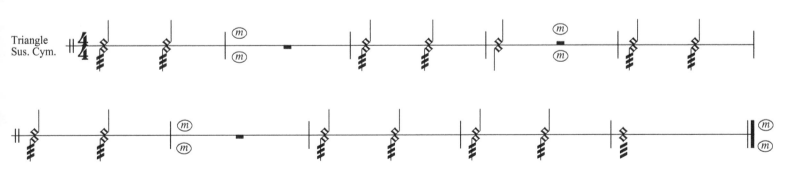

Percussion Goals

1. Breathe together and start together.
2. Match the volume of the winds.
3. Posture should be natural with the body position balanced.

5-5 Moving Down (Slurring 2 and 4)

Rolls for Xylo./Mar. only

Mallet Instruments

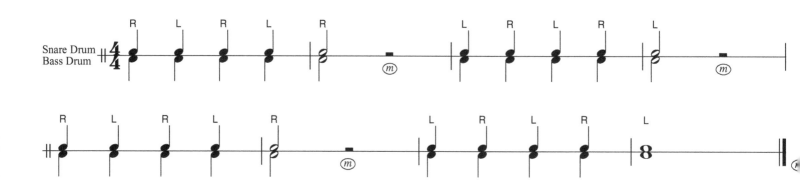

Snare Drum
Bass Drum

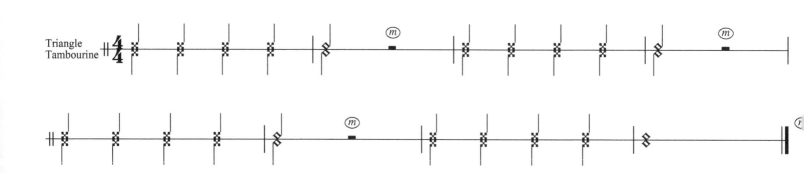

Triangle
Tambourine

Percussion Goals
1. Breathe together and start together.
2. Match the volume of the winds.
3. Posture should be natural with the body position balanced.

5-6 Moving Up (Slurring 2 and 4)

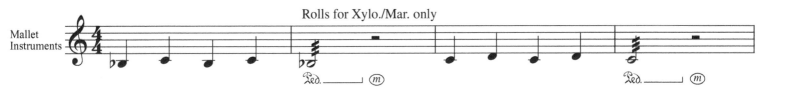

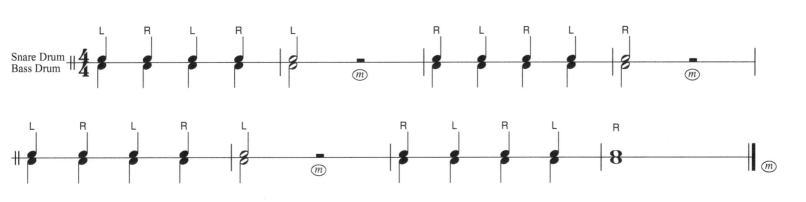

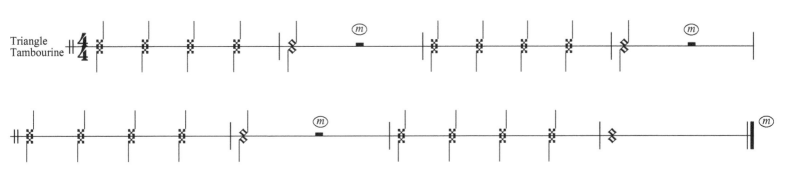

 Percussion Goals
1. Breathe together and start together.
2. Match the volume of the winds.
3. Posture should be natural with the body position balanced.

5-7 Moving Down (Slurring and Tonguing)

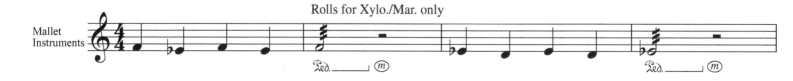

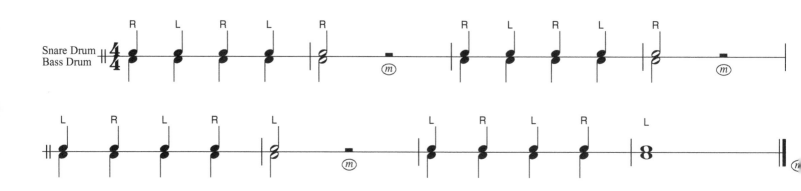

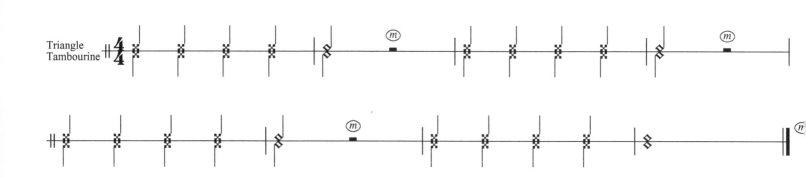

Percussion Goals

1. Breathe together and start together.
2. Match the volume of the winds.
3. Posture should be natural with the body position balanced.

5-8 Moving Up (Slurring and Tonguing)

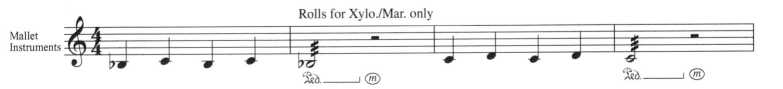

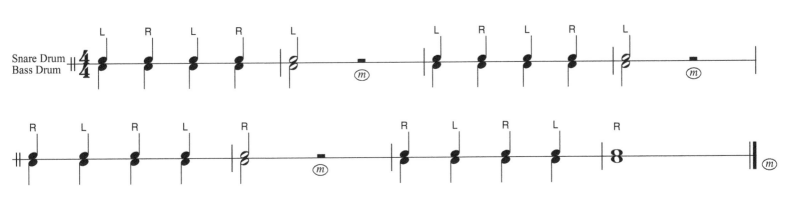

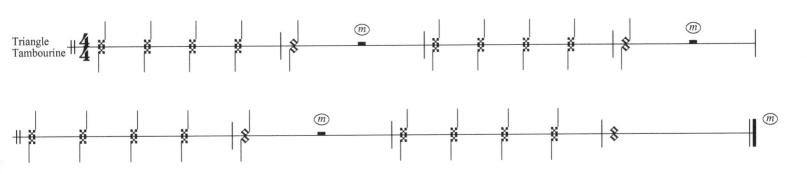

Percussion Goals
1. Breathe together and start together.
2. Match the volume of the winds.
3. Posture should be natural with the body position balanced.

6. Learning a Major Scale

Step 1

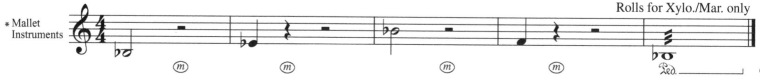

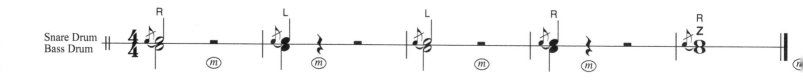

* Mallet Instruments

* Xylophone, Bells, Marimba, Vibes
🎹 (Vibes only)

Snare Drum
Bass Drum

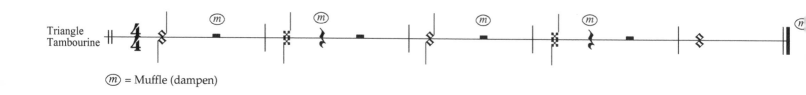

Triangle
Tambourine

(m) = Muffle (dampen)

Step 2

Mallet Instruments

Snare Drum
Bass Drum

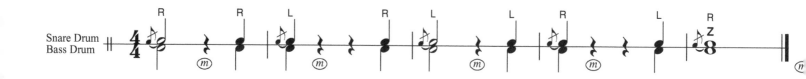

Triangle
Tambourine

Percussion Goals for Steps 1–2
1. Breathe and start together.
2. Strike the instrument in the same place
   with the same energy every time.
3. Auxiliary percussion should produce
   the same color of sound every time.

Step 3

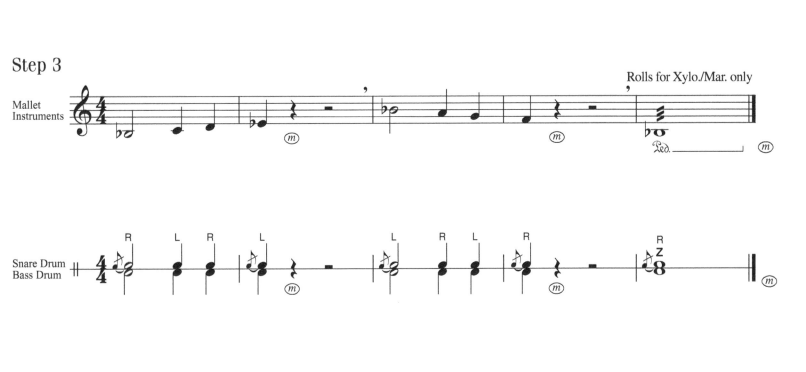

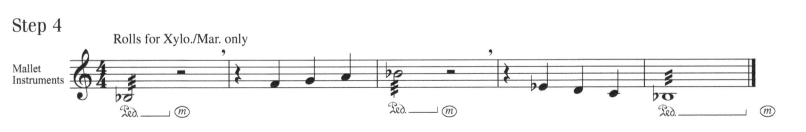

Step 4

 Percussion Goals for Steps 3–4
1. Breathe and start together.
2. Strike the instrument in the same place with the same energy every time.
3. Auxiliary percussion should produce the same color of sound every time.

Step 5

Mallet Instruments

Snare Drum
Bass Drum

Triangle
Tambourine

Percussion Goals for Step 5
1. Breathe and start together.
2. Strike the instrument in the same place with the same energy every time.
3. Auxiliary percussion should produce the same color of sound every time.

7. Learning a Chromatic Scale

7-1 Chromatic Exercise

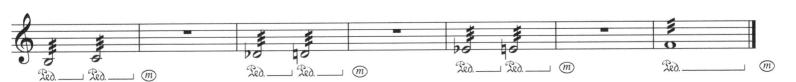

* Xylophone, Bells, Marimba, Vibes

🎹 (Vibes only)

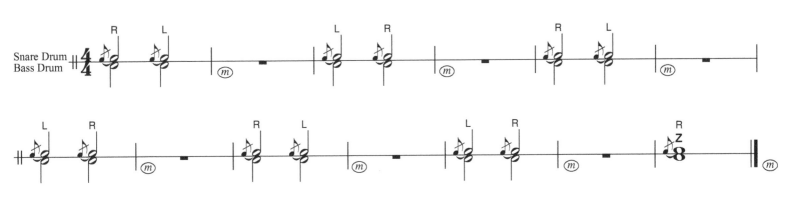

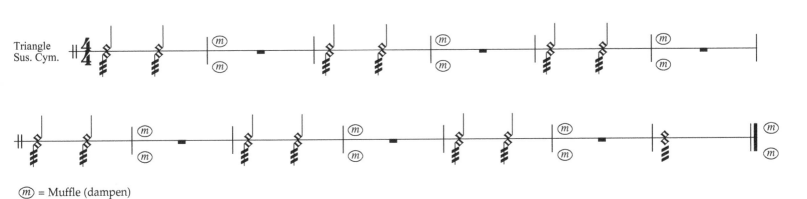

 = Muffle (dampen)

Percussion Goals
1. Breathe together and start together.
2. Strike the instrument in the same place with the same energy every time.
3. Posture should be natural with the body position balanced.

7-2 Chromatic Exercise

Mallet Instruments

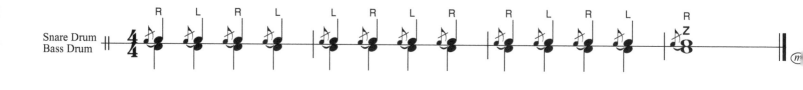

Snare Drum
Bass Drum

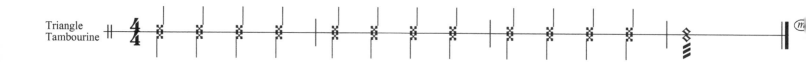

Triangle
Tambourine

Percussion Goals
1. Breathe together and start together.
2. Strike the instrument in the same place with the same energy every time.
3. Posture should be natural with the body position balanced.

7-3 Moving Up – Step 1

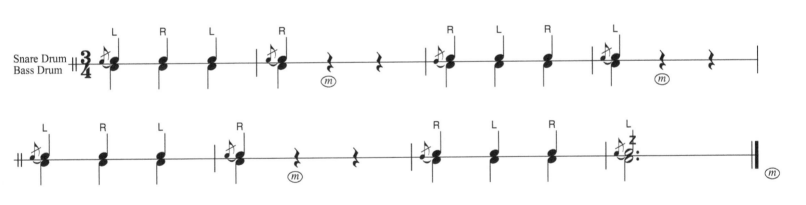

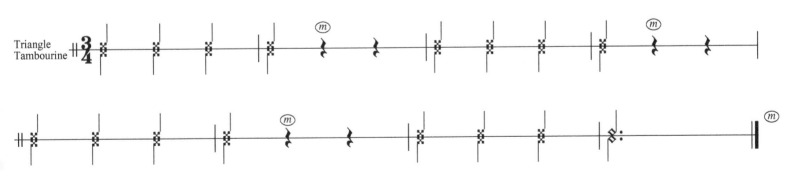

 Percussion Goals for Step 1
1. Breathe together and start together.
2. Strike the instrument in the same place with the same energy every time.
3. Posture should be natural with the body position balanced.

Step 2

Mallet
Instruments

Snare Drum
Bass Drum

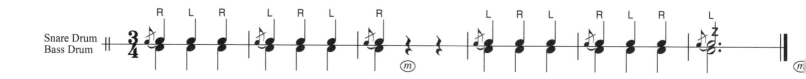

Triangle
Tambourine

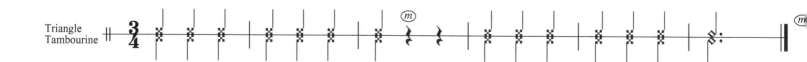

Step 3

Mallet
Instruments

Snare Drum
Bass Drum

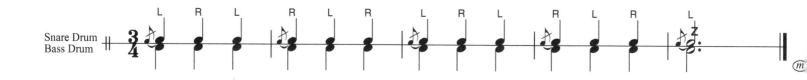

Triangle
Tambourine

Percussion Goals for Steps 2–3

1. Breathe together and start together.
2. Strike the instrument in the same place with the same energy every time.
3. Posture should be natural with the body position balanced.

-4 Moving Down

tep 1

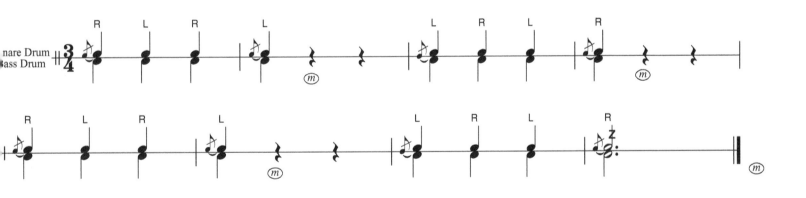

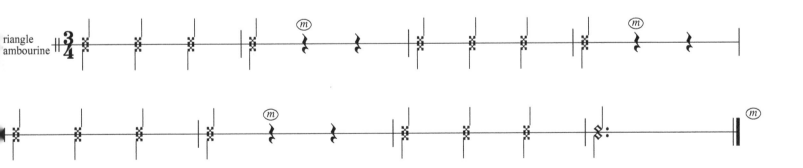

Percussion Goals for Step 1
1. Breathe together and start together.
2. Strike the instrument in the same place with the same energy every time.
3. Posture should be natural with the body position balanced.

Step 2

Mallet
Instruments

Snare Drum
Bass Drum

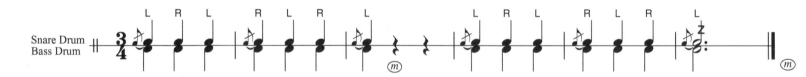

Triangle
Tambourine

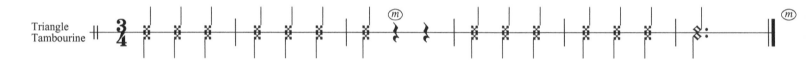

Step 3

Mallet
Instruments

Snare Drum
Bass Drum

Triangle
Tambourine

Percussion Goals for Steps 2–3

1. Breathe together and start together.
2. Strike the instrument in the same place with the same energy every time.
3. Posture should be natural with the body position balanced.